A LifeGuide®

MW00986243

GOD'S WORD
Power to Shape Our Lives

9 studies
for individuals or groups

Cindy Bunch

With Notes for Leaders

IVP Connect

An imprint of InterVarsity Press
Downers Grove, Illinois

To Jake and Margaret Zimmerman

InterVarsity Press
P.O. Box 1400, Downers Grove, IL 60515-1426
World Wide Web: www.ivpress.com
E-mail: email@ivpress.com

InterVarsity Press® *is the book-publishing division of InterVarsity Christian Fellowship/USA*®*, a student movement active on campus at hundreds of universities, colleges and schools of nursing in the United States of America, and a member movement of the International Fellowship of Evangelical Students. For information about local and regional activities, write Public Relations Dept., InterVarsity Christian Fellowship/USA, 6400 Schroeder Rd., P.O. Box 7895, Madison, WI 53707-7895, or visit the IVCF website at <www.intervarsity.org>.*

LifeGuide® *is a registered trademark of InterVarsity Christian Fellowship.*

Cover photograph: Dennis Flaherty

ISBN 978-0-8308-3092-3

Printed in the United States of America ∞

P	21	20	19	18	17	16	15	14	13	12	11	10	9	8	7	6
Y	21	20	19	18	17	16	15	14	13	12	11	10	09	08	07	

Contents

Getting the Most
Out of *God's Word*

We were gathered from across the country to discuss current Bible study models and new ways to encourage Bible study within the ministry of InterVarsity Christian Fellowship. We had spent some time discussing heady stuff like historical influences and "hermeneutical methodologies." Then our leader, Bob, opened a session by speaking from his heart about how he had experienced the power of the living Word as it is described in John 1.

"What passages have been significant for each of us in developing a love for Scripture?" someone asked. And the discussion continued. People described how God had been revealed to them through different parts of the Bible. Jean talked about how Acts 2 had helped her to understand the place of Scripture in the midst of small groups. Barry talked about passages that had shaped his call to preach. People called out their favorite chapters and verses: "Joshua 1:8," "2 Corinthians 3," "Psalm 119," "Psalm 1," "Deuteronomy 6," "2 Timothy 3."

It was a moving conversation. God had used many different passages from throughout the books of the Bible to touch us and to teach us. I wondered how this appreciation for God's Word could be passed on to others—and the idea for this guide was born.

This is not a guide about the nature of Scripture or how it was put together. It is not even a guide about how to study the Bible, though it is written out of the inductive Bible study model. *This guide is designed to bring the riches of God's living Word into our lives.* The passages in these studies will show us how Scripture comforts and encourages us and shapes us to be more like Christ.

May you discover the power of God's Word for your life in these pages.

through his Word.

2. Read the introduction to the study and respond to the personal
reflection question or exercise. This is designed to help you focus on
God and on the theme of the study.

3. Each study deals with a particular passage—so that you can
delve into the author's meaning in that context. Read and reread the
passage to be studied. The questions are written using the language of
the New International Version, so you may wish to use that version of
the Bible. The New Revised Standard Version is also recommended.

4. This is an inductive Bible study, designed to help you discover
for yourself what Scripture is saying. The study includes three types
of questions. *Observation* questions ask about the basic facts: who,
what, when, where and how. *Interpretation* questions delve into the
meaning of the passage. *Application* questions help you discover the
implications of the text for growing in Christ. These three keys
unlock the treasures of Scripture.

Write your answers to the questions in the spaces provided or in a
personal journal. Writing can bring clarity and deeper understanding
of yourself and of God's Word.

5. It might be good to have a Bible dictionary handy. Use it to look
up any unfamiliar words, names or places.

6. Use the prayer suggestion to guide you in thanking God for
what you have learned and to pray about the applications that have
come to mind.

7. You may want to go on to the suggestion under "Now or Later,"
or you may want to use that idea for your next study.

Suggestions for Members of a Group Study

1. Come to the study prepared. Follow the suggestions for individual study mentioned above. You will find that careful preparation will
greatly enrich your time spent in group discussion.

2. Be willing to participate in the discussion. The leader of your
group will not be lecturing. Instead, he or she will be encouraging the
members of the group to discuss what they have learned. The leader

will be asking the questions that are found in this guide.

3. Stick to the topic being discussed. Your answers should be based on the verses which are the focus of the discussion and not on outside authorities such as commentaries or speakers. These studies focus on a particular passage of Scripture. Only rarely should you refer to other portions of the Bible. This allows for everyone to participate in in-depth study on equal ground.

4. Be sensitive to the other members of the group. Listen attentively when they describe what they have learned. You may be surprised by their insights! Each question assumes a variety of answers. Many questions do not have "right" answers, particularly questions that aim at meaning or application. Instead the questions push us to explore the passage more thoroughly.

When possible, link what you say to the comments of others. Also, be affirming whenever you can. This will encourage some of the more hesitant members of the group to participate.

5. Be careful not to dominate the discussion. We are sometimes so eager to express our thoughts that we leave too little opportunity for others to respond. By all means participate! But allow others to also.

6. Expect God to teach you through the passage being discussed and through the other members of the group. Pray that you will have an enjoyable and profitable time together, but also that as a result of the study you will find ways that you can take action individually and/or as a group.

7. Remember that anything said in the group is considered confidential and should not be discussed outside the group unless specific permission is given to do so.

8. If you are the group leader, you will find additional suggestions at the back of the guide.

1

Longing for Christ

God's Word is alive. We experience the power of the living Word when we read Scripture and are moved to follow its teachings or when we study the Bible with others and discover new truths about faith. And when we are able to encourage others through the promises of Scripture, or—perhaps most importantly—when the eyes of seekers are opened to see the meaning of the biblical account of Christ's death and resurrection, we experience the living Word.

GROUP DISCUSSION. When and how has Scripture come to life for you?

PERSONAL REFLECTION. Spend some time thanking God for what he has taught you from Scripture thus far.

John 1 describes how the Word (God's message to the people of planet earth) was revealed to us in Christ. *Read John 1:1-5, 14-18.*

---

1. What do we learn about the Word in these verses?

2. What do God's actions in these verses reveal about his character?

3. How do you respond to this picture of Christ as the Word?

4. Why do you think the name "the Word" is used here?

5. Why is the role of the Word in creation emphasized so strongly (vv. 1-4)?

6. In what ways do people today fail to see the light shining through the darkness?

7. What do you find significant about the fact that the Word became flesh (v. 14)?

8. What are some ways that we see God's glory?

9. How can we, like John (v. 15), declare Christ's glory to others?

10. How is the law a precursor to Jesus, the Word?

11. We read in four different verses that the Word was with God. Why is this point emphasized?

12. How can regarding Scripture as God's living Word impact the way you handle it?

Ask God to be with you as you continue to study his Word and to impress his truth on your heart.

Now or Later

Read these verses in a couple different Bible versions, especially a paraphrase like *The Message* or the New Living Translation. Note the words or images that stand out. How is your understanding of this passage deepened or expanded?

2

Food for Life

My sister has recently discovered that she has a milk allergy. This means many of her favorite foods are taboo: chocolate chip cookies, pizza, mocha latte. And I have a friend who is allergic to nuts. When she eats out she always takes along an antihistamine—just in case a nut has snuck into her food. Nuts are nourishing—but for her they're also dangerous.

GROUP DISCUSSION. Tell about a time when you were not able to eat a favorite food.

Tell about a time when you were very thirsty.

PERSONAL REFLECTION. What kinds of spiritual nourishment do you need right now?

Nourishment is what Isaiah 55 is all about. It is a call to those who have been exiled from Jerusalem—a call to return and be restored to God. *Read Isaiah 55.*

1. How would you divide the passage into thematic sections, and what would you title each section?

2. Which of these invitations or promises do you find most compelling and why?

3. Who might the thirsty in verse 1 be?

4. What do we spend time and money on, only to find little satisfaction (v. 2)?

5. Does verse 6 imply that the Lord will leave us? Explain.

6. What does turning to God involve (vv. 6-7)?

7. How is God radically different from us (vv. 7-9)?

---

8. What does verse 10 reveal about God's works?

---

9. How does God's word achieve his purposes?

---

10. Look again at verses 1-10. How does verse 11 summarize all that precedes it?

---

11. Notice the promises offered to God's people in verses 12-13. How is this also the fruit of God's word?

12. What does the work of God's words as shown here reveal about the importance of studying Scripture?

13. Think back to how you answered question 2. What does this passage reveal to you about ways to find the specific spiritual nourishment you need right now?

Freely bring your needs to God. What do you hunger and thirst for?

Now or Later

Reread Isaiah 55 in a time of quiet reflection. How does God quench your hunger and thirst? Express your thanks to God in any way you feel comfortable—through prayer, poetry, dance, song, art or writing.

3

Applying the Word

Jeff preached his sermon in two languages—at the same time. He spoke aloud while he spoke through sign language. He talked about how he had learned to listen more fully, more deeply after he lost his hearing. He was free from the incessant noise of our world—free to hear God. But now he was losing his eyesight as well. Jeff was again questioning God. He felt that God was telling him that he wanted Jeff to be able to focus on him even more. Though he was honest about his fears, Jeff powerfully described a rich and deep relationship with God as all his senses drew him to experience God fully.

GROUP DISCUSSION. Have you experienced limitations in your ability to see or hear? What is that like?

PERSONAL REFLECTION. What do the senses of seeing and hearing mean to you? What would it be like to not be able to see or hear?

Jesus revealed the secrets to seeing and hearing—to those who chose to listen. *Read Matthew 13:1-23.*

1. Describe what happens to the seed in each of the four types of soil (vv. 3-8).

2. Look at the meaning of the parable in verses 18-23. If you were to cast actors to play a role that represents each of these types of soil, who would you choose and why?

3. Which type of soil do you most identify with? Explain.

4. Jesus begins answering the disciples' question about why he uses parables with the cryptic statements in verses 11-12. In verse 11 who is "you" and who is "them"?

5. In verse 12 who "has" and who "does not have"?

6. How does the quote from Isaiah in verses 14-15 clarify the statement in verse 13?

7. How have you been blessed by the opportunity to see and hear (vv. 16-17)?

8. Looking back through the passage, what do you think is being communicated about seeing and hearing Jesus?

9. When is it difficult for you to apply what you are learning from the Word?

10. What helps you to apply the Word?

11. Verse 23 speaks of the crop that comes when someone "hears the word and understands it." How have you experienced the fruit of applying the Word in your own life?

Ask God to help you to see and hear him clearly.

Now or Later

Reflect further on the metaphor of seeing and hearing. What do you need to clear out of your life so that you can see with your eyes, hear with your ears—and apply God's Word?

4

Gathering
Around the Word

Acts 2:42-47

The ages of the members vary from fourteen to forty-five. Some have gone to college, some to graduate school, and some have not pursued higher education. Careers vary from truck driver to landscape designer to preschool teacher to accountant. They come from the South, the East and the Midwest. One member attends gun shows on the weekend; another is a pacifist who protested the Gulf War. When they meet together to study the Bible the versions present include KJV, NASB, NIV, NRSV and NLV, but everyone is ready to dig in and learn from one another. This is my small group.

GROUP DISCUSSION. What different kinds of small group experiences have you had?

How have you seen the benefits of gathering with a diverse group of people?

PERSONAL REFLECTION. What have you learned from studying Scripture in small groups?

In Acts 2 the Holy Spirit comes and Peter preaches to the crowd. Verse 41 tells us that three thousand people were saved and baptized. In verses 42-47 we see what happens next in the lives of these new believers. *Read Acts 2:42-47.*

1. What qualities of the believers' fellowship do you notice throughout these verses?

2. Which of these qualities do you find appealing and why?

3. How do the elements of their life together (v. 42) help form a community?

4. How have you experienced each of these elements in your small group or church?

5. What are the results of their fellowship in their lives (vv. 43-47)?

in the lives of others?

6. How do you respond to the idea of sharing everything (vv. 44-45)?

What are some ways we can experience this aspect of community?

7. How has Christian fellowship impacted your life?

8. How have you seen Christian fellowship draw outsiders into the church?

---

9. What part does gathering around the Word through teaching and Bible study have in building Christian community?

---

10. How could you strengthen the place of the Word in communities you are a part of?

Praise God for the ways you are learning about him through experiencing the Word in the midst of community.

Now or Later

If you are not currently in a small group Bible study, make finding—or starting—a group a matter for prayer. If you are currently in a group, find ways to express appreciation for other group members. This can be done verbally, in writing or through giving small gifts.

5

Knowing
the Mind of Christ

"You deserve a break today," the McDonald's ad tells us. "Be all you can be," says the Army recruitment promotion. "Just do it" is plastered all over Nike's sportswear. Such is the wisdom of our world.

GROUP DISCUSSION. How would some of the following voices define wisdom: a skater, jock, radio disk jockey, rock star, television commercial producer, five-year-old, young mother, grandfather, or a national or international political figure?

PERSONAL REFLECTION. How would you define *wisdom?*

First Corinthians 2 shows us how the wisdom of this world contrasts sharply with the wisdom of God that helps us to know the mind of Christ. *Read 1 Corinthians 2:6-16.*

---

1. What are the different ways the word *wisdom* is used throughout this passage?

2. How does this compare with the "wisdom of this age" (v. 6)?

3. How is this view of wisdom similar to or different from how you normally think of wisdom?

4. What is God's "secret wisdom" (vv. 7-9)?

5. What comfort or encouragement does verse 9 offer you?

6. What part does God's Spirit play in showing us what wisdom is (vv. 10-13)?

How have you experienced this?

7. How do verses 12-14 highlight the deeply mysterious nature of the Spirit?

8. Verse 14 says that those without the Spirit see the things of God as foolish. How have you seen this to be true?

9. Do verses 15-16 imply that we should not allow others to teach us? Explain.

10. Drawing on this passage, what part would you say the

Spirit plays in helping us to understand Scripture?

11. Looking back through the passage, how do each of the three persons of the Trinity help us to understand God's wisdom?

12. In what ways do you need to grow in your knowledge of the mind of Christ?

Pray that the mind of Christ will be increasingly revealed to you as you study God's Word.

Now or Later

The quote in 1 Corinthians 2:9 is from Isaiah 64. Read that chapter. Confess any sin that comes to mind in response to these verses. Thank God for his promise to help (v. 5).

6

Guided by the Word

In *Confessions* Augustine writes about how certain books of the Bible guided him at a time when he was struggling with sin.

> These books served to remind me to return to my own self. Under your guidance I entered into the depths of my own soul, and this I was able to do because *your aid befriended me* [Psalm 29:11]. . . .
>
> I realized I was far away from you. It was as though I were in a land where all is different from your own and I heard your voice calling from on high saying "I am the food of full-grown men. Grow and you shall feed on me." (R. S. Pine-Coffin, trans. [New York: Penguin, 1961], pp. 146-47)

Whether we are in the midst of sin, relational difficulties or a major life transition, the Word of God is one resource God has given us for guidance.

GROUP DISCUSSION. What is one of the hardest decisions you've ever had to make? What process did you go through to make that decision?

PERSONAL REFLECTION. What decision is currently troubling

you? Take time to put that before God as you begin this study.

Psalm 119 is an extended reflection on God's law and commandments and the teachings in his Word. It is a source of inspiration to us to spend time studying Scripture. *Read Psalm 119:97-108.*

1. What different words and phrases are used to describe God's Word?

2. Which of these do you identify with from your own experience of studying Scripture?

3. How has studying God's Word benefited the writer of this psalm?

4. Notice verse 98. You may or may not feel that you have "enemies," but how does God's Word make you better able to face those who stand against God?

5. What do you think the writer is trying to communicate through the comparisons of his understanding to that of his teachers and of the elders (vv. 99-100)?

6. How has God's Word shaped and formed you?

7. Verse 103 describes God's Word as having a sweet taste. What does this metaphor mean to you?

8. How does Scripture light our pathways?

Give an example of a situation in which you have experienced
this.

---

9. How does God's Word give us life in the midst of our suffer-
ing (v. 107)?

---

10. The author responds to these reflections on Scripture by
offering God his praise. How do you feel about God after
studying this passage?

Offer your praise to God for the sweetness of his Word.

Now or Later

The author speaks of making Scripture his meditation all day
long (v. 97). Set aside time to meditate on portions of this passage or other parts of Psalm 119. Begin by asking God to clear
your mind of the day's troubles. Then just read through a section several times noting the verses that strike you. Make those
verses a focus of continued prayer and reflection, asking God
for his leading.

7

Strengthened by the Word

Attending childbirth preparation classes was a stomach-tightening, nauseating experience. Hearing the details week after week of how the baby would emerge, what could go wrong and what we had to do in the process increased our anxiety rather than lessening it. It seemed to have the same effect on others in the class. At one point when the teacher was showing us a dilation chart illustrating the dramatic change that would take place, a lawyer in the class chose to cross-examine. Pointing at the chart, she said, "You are saying we have to go from there to there. That seems highly improbable!"

GROUP DISCUSSION. Describe a time when you faced a task that seemed impossible. What gave you the courage to move forward?

PERSONAL REFLECTION. When is it hard for you to have courage?

Moses has led the people out of enslavement in Egypt and on their desert journey for forty years. Now Joshua faces the daunting task of replacing Moses and leading the Israelites into the next part of God's plan. God exhorts Joshua to be coura-geous, pointing him to the Word as a source of strength and comfort. *Read Joshua 1:1-9.*

---

1. In this passage, what is God asking Joshua to do?

---

2. What does God promise Joshua?

---

3. What thoughts and feelings would Joshua have had as he heard God's plan for him?

---

4. In what area of your life do you need to be strong and coura-geous?

5. What does it mean to not turn "to the right or to the left" of God's law?

6. How is the "Book of the Law" to be a help to Joshua?

7. The "Book of the Law" was an early portion of Scripture. What do you learn from verse 8 about how we should treat God's Word?

What are some ways we could make the practices mentioned in verse 8 more a part of our lives?

8. How does God's Word give you courage when you face challenging circumstances?

_____

9. Read verse 9 again. How could you use the message of this verse to encourage someone?

Pray for God's strength and courage to become a part of your character and actions.

Now or Later

Pick a verse or two to memorize and meditate on so that God's Word will not "depart from your mouth."

8

Passing the Word On

We were all gathered to plan the funeral of Eula Montgomery, my husband's grandmother. We were almost finished discussing the service, when the pastor asked what text the family would like him to use for the sermon. Favorite passages were named. Then her granddaughter Angela mentioned 2 Timothy 1:5: "I have been reminded of your sincere faith, which first lived in your grandmother Lois and in your mother Eunice and, I am persuaded, now lives in you also." That seemed like an ideal selection to honor a woman who had the courage to *start* teaching a Sunday school class when she was in her eighties.

GROUP DISCUSSION. Has anyone in your family or your church nurtured your faith? Tell a little about that person.

PERSONAL REFLECTION. Spend time praying your thanks for those who have nurtured your faith.

The book of Deuteronomy is made up of Moses' last words to the Israelites. Moses reminds the Israelites of the Ten Commandments and other laws throughout this book as they are planning to enter the Promised Land. Moses will not go with them. *Read Deuteronomy 6:1-9.*

1. What do you think the Israelites were thinking and feeling as Moses gave these instructions?

2. What strong words do you notice as you read through this passage?

Why do you think Moses chose to express himself in this way?

3. Focus on verse 2. What faith traditions and beliefs have you seen passed along in your extended family?

4. What are the rewards (v. 3) that we can see in our culture for obeying verse 2?

5. Notice the truths that are stressed in verses 4-5. Why are these particular teachings to be "on our hearts" (v. 6)?

6. Consider verses 6-9 as a unit. Each verse describes a different action. What are they?

7. How can the truths of Scripture be integrated into our lives in the way that's described in verse 7?

8. How can we display the truths of Scripture outwardly as described in verse 8?

9. How can God's Word be recognizable on (or in) our houses?

10. What are the key aspects of faith that you would like to pass on to the younger generations you have an opportunity to influence?

How can you be more effective in doing that?

Pray for an opportunity to talk to a younger Christian about your faith.

Now or Later

Read Paul's testimony to Timothy in 2 Timothy 3:10-17. How has Scripture "thoroughly equipped" you "for every good work"? Be ready to share this testimony with someone else.

9

Reflecting the Word

2 Corinthians 3

Retreats, camps and conferences can be life-changing events. My friend Jen wrote the following letter to describe her growth at a national youth gathering.

> Ya know that conference meant the world to me. It really did. It opened my eyes to a lot of things. But I think the wierdest thing about it is that if I died today or tomorrow, I'd be content about my life. And I've never been able to say that before. But now I really can.

GROUP DISCUSSION. Describe a mountaintop experience you've had—a time when you grew in Christ significantly. Try to recapture what you felt.

PERSONAL REFLECTION. Recall a time when reading God's Word met a specific need or opened a certain area of growth for you.

In his letters to the Corinthians, Paul talks about how Scripture shapes us and allows us to reflect the image of God at work within us. *Read 2 Corinthians 3.*

1. In what different ways is the word *letter* used in verses 1-7?

2. Who could serve as your "letter of recommendation"?

3. Verse 6 says, "The letter kills, but the Spirit gives life." How have you seen this to be true? (Give an example.)

4. What implications does verse 6 have for how we read and apply Scripture?

5. What is the ministry that "brought death" (v. 7)?

What do we learn from how it is contrasted with the "ministry of the Spirit" (vv. 8-11)?

6. How does the Word make you bold (v. 12)?

7. Trace the different ways the veil is used in verses 13-18.

8. What do you think is the meaning of the veil for people today?

9. Receiving God's law caused Moses to reflect God's glory. How can God's Word cause us to reflect God's glory?

10. We began by thinking of extraordinary experiences we've had with God. How can spending time with God and his Word impact your everyday life?

11. How do you plan to allow the Word to continue to shape you, making you into a letter from Christ?

Ask God to shape you with his Word.

Now or Later

What are your goals for continued reading, meditation and study? How often do you want to spend time in God's Word? for what time period? What new study methods would you like to try? Spend time in prayer (and discussion if you are in a group) as you make a plan for yourself.

Leader's Notes

Leading a Bible discussion can be an enjoyable and rewarding experience. But it can also be *scary*—especially if you've never done it before. If this is your feeling, you're in good company. When God asked Moses to lead the Israelites out of Egypt, he replied, "O Lord, please send someone else to do it"! (Ex 4:13). It was the same with Solomon, Jeremiah and Timothy, but God helped these people in spite of their weaknesses, and he will help you as well.

You don't need to be an expert on the Bible or a trained teacher to lead a Bible discussion. The idea behind these inductive studies is that the leader guides group members to discover for themselves what the Bible has to say. This method of learning will allow group members to remember much more of what is said than a lecture would.

These studies are designed to be led easily. As a matter of fact, the flow of questions through the passage from observation to interpretation to application is so natural that you may feel that the studies lead themselves. This study guide is also flexible. You can use it with a variety of groups—student, professional, neighborhood or church groups. Each study takes forty-five to sixty minutes in a group setting.

There are some important facts to know about group dynamics and encouraging discussion. The suggestions listed below should enable you to effectively and enjoyably fulfill your role as leader.

Preparing for the Study

1. Ask God to help you understand and apply the passage in your own life. Unless this happens, you will not be prepared to lead others. Pray too for the various members of the group. Ask God to open your hearts to the message of his Word and motivate you to action.

2. Read the introduction to the entire guide to get an overview of the entire book and the issues which will be explored.

3. As you begin each study, read and reread the assigned Bible passage to familiarize yourself with it.

4. This study guide is based on the New International Version of the Bible. It will help you and the group if you use this translation as the basis for your study and discussion.

5. Carefully work through each question in the study. Spend time in meditation and reflection as you consider how to respond.

6. Write your thoughts and responses in the space provided in the study guide. This will help you to express your understanding of the passage clearly.

7. It might help to have a Bible dictionary handy. Use it to look up any unfamiliar words, names or places. (For additional help on how to study a passage, see chapter five of *How to Lead a LifeGuide Bible Study,* InterVarsity Press.)

8. Consider how you can apply the Scripture to your life. Remember that the group will follow your lead in responding to the studies. They will not go any deeper than you do.

9. Once you have finished your own study of the passage, familiarize yourself with the leader's notes for the study you are leading. These are designed to help you in several ways. First, they tell you the purpose the study guide author had in mind when writing the study. Take time to think through how the study questions work together to accomplish that purpose. Second, the notes provide you with additional background information or suggestions on group dynamics for various questions. This information can be useful when people have difficulty understanding or answering a question. Third, the leader's notes can alert you to potential problems you may encounter during the study.

10. If you wish to remind yourself of anything mentioned in the leader's notes, make a note to yourself below that question in the study.

Leading the Study

1. Begin the study on time. Open with prayer, asking God to help the group to understand and apply the passage.

2. Be sure that everyone in your group has a study guide. Encourage the group to prepare beforehand for each discussion by reading the introduction to the guide and by working through the questions in the study.

3. At the beginning of your first time together, explain that these studies are meant to be discussions, not lectures. Encourage the members of the group to participate. However, do not put pressure on those who may be hesitant to speak during the first few sessions. You may want to suggest the following guidelines to your group.

☐ Stick to the topic being discussed.

☐ Your responses should be based on the verses which are the focus of the discussion and not on outside authorities such as commentaries or speakers.

☐ These studies focus on a particular passage of Scripture. Only rarely should you refer to other portions of the Bible. This allows for everyone to participate in in-depth study on equal ground.

☐ Anything said in the group is considered confidential and will not be discussed outside the group unless specific permission is given to do so.

☐ We will listen attentively to each other and provide time for each person present to talk.

☐ We will pray for each other.

4. Have a group member read the introduction at the beginning of the discussion.

5. Every session begins with a group discussion question. The question or activity is meant to be used before the passage is read. The question introduces the theme of the study and encourages group members to begin to open up. Encourage as many members as possible to participate, and be ready to get the discussion going with your own response.

This section is designed to reveal where our thoughts or feelings need to be transformed by Scripture. That is why it is especially important not to read the passage before the discussion question is asked. The passage will tend to color the honest reactions people would otherwise give because they are, of course, supposed to think the way the Bible does.

You may want to supplement the group discussion question with an icebreaker to help people to get comfortable. See the community section of *Small Group Idea Book* for more ideas.

You also might want to use the personal reflection question with your group. Either allow a time of silence for people to respond individually or discuss it together.

6. Have a group member (or members if the passage is long) read aloud the passage to be studied. Then give people several minutes to read the passage again silently so that they can take it all in.

7. Question 1 will generally be an overview question designed to briefly survey the passage. Encourage the group to look at the whole passage, but try to avoid getting sidetracked by questions or issues that will be addressed later in the study.

8. As you ask the questions, keep in mind that they are designed to be used just as they are written. You may simply read them aloud. Or you may prefer to express them in your own words.

There may be times when it is appropriate to deviate from the study guide. For example, a question may have already been answered. If so, move on to the next question. Or someone may raise an important question not covered in the guide. Take time to discuss it, but try to keep the group from going off on tangents.

9. Avoid answering your own questions. If necessary, repeat or rephrase them until they are clearly understood. Or point out something you read in the leader's notes to clarify the context or meaning. An eager group quickly becomes passive and silent if they think the leader will do most of the talking.

10. Don't be afraid of silence. People may need time to think about the question before formulating their answers.

11. Don't be content with just one answer. Ask, "What do the rest of you think?" or "Anything else?" until several people have given answers to the question.

12. Acknowledge all contributions. Try to be affirming whenever possible. Never reject an answer. If it is clearly off-base, ask, "Which verse led you to that conclusion?" or again, "What do the rest of you think?"

13. Don't expect every answer to be addressed to you, even though this will probably happen at first. As group members become more at ease, they will begin to truly interact with each other. This is one sign of healthy discussion.

14. Don't be afraid of controversy. It can be very stimulating. If you don't resolve an issue completely, don't be frustrated. Move on and keep it in mind for later. A subsequent study may solve the problem.

15. Periodically summarize what the group has said about the passage. This helps to draw together the various ideas mentioned and gives continuity to the study. But don't preach.

16. At the end of the Bible discussion you may want to allow group members a time of quiet to work on an idea under "Now or Later." Then discuss what you experienced. Or you may want to encourage group members to work on these ideas between meetings. Give an opportunity during the session for people to talk about what they are learning.

17. Conclude your time together with conversational prayer, adapting the prayer suggestion at the end of the study to your group. Ask for God's help in following through on the commitments you've made.

18. End on time.

Many more suggestions and helps are found in *How to Lead a LifeGuide Bible Study.*

Components of Small Groups
A healthy small group should do more than study the Bible. There are four components to consider as you structure your time together.

Nurture. Small groups help us to grow in our knowledge and love of God. Bible study is the key to making this happen and is the foundation of your small group.

Community. Small groups are a great place to develop deep friendships with other Christians. Allow time for informal interaction before and after each study. Plan activities and games that will help you get to know each other. Spend time having fun together—going on a picnic or cooking dinner together.

Worship and prayer. Your study will be enhanced by spending time praising God together in prayer or song. Pray for each other's needs—and keep track of how God is answering prayer in your group. Ask God to help you to apply what you are learning in your study.

Outreach. Reaching out to others can be a practical way of applying what you are learning, and it will keep your group from becoming self-focused. Host a series of evangelistic discussions for your friends or neighbors. Clean up the yard of an elderly friend. Serve at a soup kitchen together, or spend a day working on a Habitat house.

Many more suggestions and helps in each of these areas are found in *Small Group Idea Book.* Information on building a small group can be found in *Small Group Leaders' Handbook* and *The Big Book on Small Groups* (both from InterVarsity Press). Reading through one of these books would be worth your time.

Study 1. Longing for Christ. John 1:1-5, 14-18.

Purpose: To discover how we meet Christ in the living Word of Scripture.

Group discussion. Use this question to orient the group to the topic—before reading the passage. Encourage as many as possible to respond.

Personal reflection. These questions are designed for individuals studying on their own. However, you can use them with a group by giving members a few minutes to reflect quietly before they begin the study. You may find some suitable for group discussion as well. Use them as you wish.

Question 1. This question is designed to give a brief overview of the themes of the passage. We'll go into more detail on each verse later, so don't dwell on this too long.

Question 4. If people find this difficult, you may want to read the following quote from *The NIV Study Bible* and discuss it.

> Greeks used this term not only of the spoken word but also of the unspoken word, the word still in the mind—the reason. When they applied it to the universe, they meant the rational principle that governs all things. Jews, on the other hand, used it as a way of referring to God. Thus John used a term that was meaningful to both Jews and Gentiles. (Kenneth Barker, ed. [Grand Rapids, Mich.: Zondervan, 1995], p. 1590.)

Question 5. Note in Genesis 1 how, as God speaks, each aspect of the world comes into being. We may think of a word as passive ink on a page, but this is a Word with power—the power to bring us into existence.

Study 2. Food for Life. Isaiah 55.

Purpose: To hear the invitation to be nourished and sustained by the Word.

Question 1. The sections are verses 1-2, 3-5, 6-9, 10-11 and 12-13.

Question 3. In these verses Isaiah "brings before us the worldwide consequences of the Servant's work. . . . The whole world [is] invited into the new world" (Alec Motyer, *Isaiah*, Tyndale Old Testament Commentaries [Downers Grove, Ill.: InterVarsity Press, 1999], p. 343).

Question 5. Alec Motyer suggests that the meaning of *seek* is

> not to look for something lost but to come with diligence to where the Lord is to be found. It speaks, therefore, of commitment, determination, persistence in spiritual concern and in longing for the Lord's presence and fellowship. (*Isaiah*, p. 345)

Question 6. "Seeking" God is the first step. "Calling" involves worshiping God and appealing to him in need. Motyer says, "*Forsake* and *turn* are the two sides of true repentance, turning from and turning to (1 Thes. 1:9)." "Ways" refers to lifestyle ("as when we excuse somebody for being rude by saying, 'He doesn't mean it. It's just his way'"). "Thoughts" refers to the mindset that plans the lifestyle. "Mercy" involves being "embraced in a surge of divine love" (*Isaiah*, p. 345).

Question 9. According to Motyer,

> The Word of God—in our privileged day, the Holy Scriptures—comes from the Lord himself and is the Lord's chosen instrument to achieve his purposes. The Bible reveals his thoughts and ways, sets his targets, voices his promises and is powerful to achieve what it expresses. . . . In this passage the focus is narrower. It speaks particularly of the divine word heard in the call to repentance, the command to come back to God. (*Isaiah*, p. 346)

Question 11. If time allows, you might ask people to list the promises and what they mean in more concrete spiritual and emotional terms.

Question 13. You may need to brainstorm beyond the text to help people take steps toward finding spiritual nourishment.

Study 3. Applying the Word. Matthew 13:1-23.

Purpose: To be motivated by the parable of the sower to both hear and respond to God's Word.

Group discussion. If people don't think this applies to them, remind them what it's like to have your pupils dilated. Or think about how things sound when you get off a plane and your ears are ringing.

Questions 1-2. The four types of soil are as follows: (1) verses 3-4, (2) verses 5-6, (3) verse 7, and (4) verse 8. These four are paralleled by (1) verse 19, (2) verses 20-21, (3) verse 22, and (4) verse 23.

Question 4. Craig Keener notes, "Jesus emphasizes that only his inner circle will understand, because the parables make sense only in the context of Jesus' ministry. . . . only those who press into his inner circle, those who persevere to mature discipleship, will prove to be good soil" (*Matthew*, IVP New Testament Commentary [Downers Grove, Ill.: InterVarsity Press, 1997], p. 236).

Question 5. Notice that while Jesus started out speaking to a large crowd, now it is the disciples who are crowded around him. "To those who had some revelation, more revelation would be given (Mt 13:11-12). In other words, the disciples alone proved to be good soil (v. 23)" (Keener, *Matthew*, p. 239).

Question 6. If you want to look at the background text, the source of the quote in verses 14-15 is Isaiah 6:9-10.

Question 8. Review references to seeing and hearing in verse 2 where the crowd is listening to Jesus, as well in verses 9, 13, 14-15, 16-17 and 18-23.

Study 4. Gathering Around the Word. Acts 2:42-47.

Purpose: To discover the place of the Word at the center of Christian community, drawing us together as we learn about God.

Question 3. Consider each of the elements listed in verse 42: teaching (or Bible study), fellowship (including eating together) and prayer.

Question 4. If it has not already been covered, you might follow up by asking, "How do these elements balance each other?"

This question could bring out feelings of disappointment and disgruntlement that may not be productive. If the conversation goes this way, encourage members to think of ways they can bring about change by taking these elements to a church or small group.

Question 5. Notice the miracles (v. 43), the giving and sharing (vv. 44-45), the spiritual growth (they worshiped "with glad

and sincere hearts," v. 46) and the evangelistic outreach (v. 47).
Question 6. Allow people to react to this idea, which may seem surprising or extreme. But don't let the potentially intimidating idea of sharing *everything* keep you from seeing how you might share *something*. Consider ideas like loaning a car to someone, getting a group together to paint someone's house or opening your home to a missionary on sabbatical.
Question 8. Reflect on different types of small groups or Sunday school classes you have been in. How has Scripture played a meaningful part in those groups?
Question 9. Again, focus on what individuals can do rather than on the problems they may have experienced.
Now or Later. If you are leading a group, this is a good time to express appreciation for one another. One fun way to do this incorporates a ball of yarn. With the group sitting in a circle, the leader ties the yarn to a wrist and then tosses it to another member, expressing appreciation for something about that person. The second person wraps the yarn around his or her wrist and then tosses it to a third person with a word of appreciation. At the end lift your hands (you can have each person get involved once or twice), and you'll see how Christ's love weaves us together.

Study 5. Knowing the Mind of Christ. 1 Corinthians 2:6-16.
Purpose: To understand the work of the Spirit through the Word to give us understanding of the "things of God."
Group discussion. You might want to give out slips of paper with one of the categories written on each. Ask each person to speak in the voice listed. See if the rest of the group can guess who they are. So the disk jockey might say, "We're looking for callers who can tell us how to get out of a relationship after a one-night stand." The idea here is to show the world's wisdom, not biblical wisdom. If time is short, you may want to simplify

by just discussing a couple categories together.

General note. Notice how Paul begins chapter 2 by minimizing his "eloquence or superior wisdom." *The NIV Study Bible* suggests that Paul may have been minimizing the influence of Apollos, who put too much emphasis on human wisdom (p. 1738).

Question 1. In verse 6 "philosophers used the term for 'mature' or 'perfect' (KJV) . . . for those who had progressed to an advanced stage in wisdom" (Craig S. Keener, *The IVP Bible Background Commentary: New Testament* [Downers Grove, Ill.: InterVarsity Press, 1993], p. 457).

Question 4. See Ephesians 3:4-6 regarding the "secret."

Question 6. With the first part of the question, note what the text has to say. Then push beyond this for deeper interpretation by discussing experiences group members have had of having the Spirit help them understand the meaning of the text.

The IVP Bible Background Commentary has a helpful comment:

> Only God's Spirit knows what is in his heart, but because believers have God's Spirit, they can know his heart too. This was a radical statement for most of ancient Judaism, because most Jewish teachers did not believe that the Spirit was active in their day. "Spirit" had a broad variety of meanings, including "attitude," "disposition"; hence "spirit of the world" need not refer to any particular spiritual being (unlike God's Spirit). (p. 458)

Question 11. Use this question to summarize the passage and draw out some principles for how God gives us wisdom.

Study 6. Guided by the Word. Psalm 119:97-108.

Purpose: To learn how the Word guides our choices in life.

Personal reflection. A decision of some sort is usually nagging at us. If you are leading a group, you may want to allow a few minutes for people to think about or pray through this question as you begin. Or you could come back to it at the end, perhaps praying in twos.

Question 1. Notice "law" and "laws"(vv. 97, 102, 108), "commands" (v. 98), "statutes" (v. 99), "precepts" (vv. 100, 104), "sweet" and "sweeter than honey" (v. 103), "lamp" and "light" (v. 105). If the group misses some of these, point to the specific verses and ask them what they see there.

Question 3. Draw responses to this question from the text. Notice "wiser than my enemies" (v. 98), "more insight than all my teachers" (v. 99), "more understanding than the elders" (v. 100), "kept my feet from every evil path" (v. 101), "not departed from your laws" (v. 102), and "gain understanding" and "hate every wrong path" (v. 104).

Question 6. Examples may be cited out of what you observed in questions 3 through 5 or simply from personal experience.

Question 8. To get the group started talking, be ready to offer an example of how Scripture has given you direction in the midst of a difficult decision.

Study 7. Strengthened by the Word. Joshua 1:1-9.

Purpose: To see how the Word gives us boldness to follow God into new territory.

Group discussion. Answers to this don't have to be deeply serious to get people started thinking about facing challenges in life. They can include new tasks at work or the requirements of sports and hobbies.

Background. See Deuteronomy 31:1-8 for the story of how God chose Joshua.

Question 1. Notice actions and character qualities (vv. 6-7).

Question 2. According to *The NIV Study Bible*, "The dimensions of the land promised to Israel vary (compare this text and Ge 15:18 with Dt 34:1-4), but these are the farthest limits— conquered and held only by David and Solomon" (p. 289).

Question 3. These verses are the point of transition between the story of Moses in Deuteronomy and God's appointing of Joshua. According to Trent C. Butler, there are five major components to Israelite leadership. (1) "All leadership in Israel occurs in the shadow of Moses." (2) The leader's task is "to maintain the land for himself and his fellows." (3) God's presence is promised. (4) But the leader must be obedient to the Law given to Moses. (5) God "called the leader to reflect upon and respond to the divine word" (*Joshua*, Word Biblical Commentary [Waco, Tex.: Word, 1983], pp. 13-14).

Question 6. The "Book of the Law" is a reference to the law of Moses given by God to Moses in Deuteronomy 4:44—26:19.

Question 7. According to *The NIV Study Bible,* there was already a "documentary form of the laws from Sinai," but the "law was usually read orally." See, for example, Deuteronomy 30:9-14 (p. 289). For us, keeping the Word in our mouths can also mean speaking it to one another and speaking from hearts and minds nourished by the Word.

Study 8. Passing the Word On. Deuteronomy 6:1-9.

Purpose: To discover our part in teaching the next generation to love the Word.

General note. The study and questions have been designed to apply to those who have children and those who don't. Be sensitive to the makeup of your group and help people to make the application. We all influence the younger generation in some ways.

Group discussion. Be sensitive to the fact that some members won't have Christians in their families. A few responses will be sufficient.

Question 2. Notice "commands," "decrees," "laws" and "commandments." And "teach" and "impress." Also "observe," "obey" and "keep."

Question 3. "Faith traditions" can include all sorts of actions and teachings. It could be passing down a Bible when a child turns twelve. Perhaps someone comes from an atheistic family. Their faith tradition might be going to church once a year—at Christmas. Some may have experienced traditions from other faiths as well.

Question 7. Think about ways you learn Scripture in your home: family devotions, memory verses, discussing Sunday school lessons and take-home papers, praying the Lord's Prayer.

Question 8. This is not necessarily an endorsement for Christian T-shirts. Hopefully our speech and actions will reflect our faith to the world.

Question 9. Scripture might be displayed in our homes in a picture or wall hanging. The teachings of Scripture can also be apparent in how we welcome people into our homes, whether we choose furnishings for comfort or for show, and so on.

Study 9. Reflecting the Word. 2 Corinthians 3.
Purpose: To see how our lives are a testament of the work of the Word. Like Christ, we are the living Word.

Question 1. This question is designed to get people reading and surveying the text. The next several questions will dig more deeply into the meanings of "letter."

Question 2. Some may feel that answering this question is "bragging on themselves." Remind them that Paul speaks very clearly and boldly in verses 2-3. He is not embarrassed to speak about how God has used him to reach others. We should not be either.

Question 3. Linda Belleville says,

> What is qualitatively better about the new covenant is that it is not a *letter* covenant—that is, an external code—but a *Spirit* covenant—that is, internal power. A covenant that is *letter* in

nature *kills* because it makes external demands without giving the inward power for obedience, while a covenant that is *Spirit* in character *gives life* because it works internally to produce a change of nature. (2 *Corinthians*, IVP New Testament Commentary [Downers Grove, Ill.: InterVarsity Press, 1996, pp. 94-95)

Question 5. Belleville says of the Mosaic covenant: "Far from being the key to the victorious Christian life, it is in reality a ministry that brings nothing but *death* (v. 7) and condemnation (v. 9) to those of God's people who strive to live by it. To be a minister of the old covenant is therefore to be an instrument of death and destruction. The new covenant ministry, on the other hand, brings *the Spirit* (v. 8) and *righteousness* (v. 9)" (2 *Corinthians*, p. 97).

Question 7. "The veil" is a reference to Exodus 34:33-35.

Question 8. Belleville points out the shift from the plural "they" in verse 15 to the singular "anyone" in verse 16. "In spite of national blindness—which explains why Israel as a whole is not responding to the gospel—there is still the possibility of a personal response" (2 *Corinthians*, p. 109).

Cindy Bunch is a senior editor at InterVarsity Press. She is also the author of the LifeGuide® Bible Studies Christian Virtues *and* A Woman of God.

What Should We Study Next?

A good place to continue your study of Scripture would be with a book study. Many groups begin with a Gospel such as *Mark* (20 studies by Jim Hoover) or *John* (26 studies by Douglas Connelly). These guides are divided into two parts so that if twenty or twenty-six weeks seems like too much to do at once, the group can feel free to do half and take a break with another topic. Later you might want to come back to it. You might prefer to try a shorter letter. *Philippians* (9 studies by Donald Baker), *Ephesians* (11 studies by Andrew T. and Phyllis J. Le Peau) and *1 & 2 Timothy and Titus* (12 studies by Pete Sommer) are good options. If you want to vary your reading with an Old Testament book, consider *Ecclesiastes* (12 studies by Bill and Teresa Syrios) for a challenging and exciting study.

There are a number of interesting topical LifeGuide studies as well. Here are some options for filling three or four quarters of a year:

Basic Discipleship
Christian Beliefs, 12 studies by Stephen D. Eyre
Christian Character, 12 studies by Andrea Sterk & Peter Scazzero
Christian Disciplines, 12 studies by Andrea Sterk & Peter Scazzero
Evangelism, 12 studies by Rebecca Pippert & Ruth Siemens

Building Community
Christian Community, 12 studies by Rob Suggs
Fruit of the Spirit, 9 studies by Hazel Offner
Spiritual Gifts, 12 studies by Charles & Anne Hummel

Character Studies
New Testament Characters, 12 studies by Carolyn Nystrom
Old Testament Characters, 12 studies by Peter Scazzero
Old Testament Kings, 12 studies by Carolyn Nystrom
Women of the Old Testament, 12 studies by Gladys Hunt

The Trinity
Meeting God, 12 studies by J. I. Packer
Meeting Jesus, 13 studies by Leighton Ford
Meeting the Spirit, 12 studies by Douglas Connelly